A
HISTORY
of
TOUCH

FIRST POETS SERIES 22

Guernica Editions Inc. acknowledges the support of
the Canada Council for the Arts and the Ontario Arts Council.
The Ontario Arts Council is an agency of the Government of Ontario.
We acknowledge the financial support of the Government of Canada

Erin Emily Ann Vance

A

HISTORY

of

TOUCH

GUERNICA
EDITIONS

TORONTO • CHICAGO • BUFFALO • LANCASTER (U.K.)
2022

Guernica Founder: Antonio D'Alfonso

Michael Mirolla, general editor
Elana Wolff, editor
Cover and Interior design: Rafael Chimicatti
Guernica Editions Inc.
287 Templemead Drive, Hamilton, ON L8W 2W4
2250 Military Road, Tonawanda, N.Y. 14150-6000 U.S.A.
www.guernicaeditions.com

Distributors:
Independent Publishers Group (IPG)
600 North Pulaski Road, Chicago IL 60624
University of Toronto Press Distribution (UTP)
5201 Dufferin Street, Toronto (ON), Canada M3H 5T8
Gazelle Book Services, White Cross Mills
High Town, Lancaster LA1 4XS U.K.

First edition.
Printed in Canada.

Legal Deposit—First Quarter
Library of Congress Catalog Card Number: 2021953544
Library and Archives Canada Cataloguing in Publication
Title: A history of touch / Erin Emily Ann Vance.
Names: Vance, Erin Emily Ann, author.
Series: First poets series (Toronto, Ont.) ; 22.
Description: Series statement: First poets series ; 22
Identifiers: Canadiana 20220136580 | ISBN 9781771837217 (softcover)
Classification: LCC PS8643.A68745 H57 2022 | DDC C811/.6—dc23

For my grandmother, Ann Lakes

CONTENTS

I.

II.

III.

I.

"This is the marrow of the house."

ALL THE WOMEN YOU'VE EVER TOUCHED

You want to leave me to rot?
Fine.

Let my hair burn into copper moss
in the forest saw off chunks of my flesh.
I am not far from the window, so
lick me fat like a silkworm.

Suck on my rotting eyes, forget
that they are the eyes of your mother.
Drink the bile that lingers;
it will go well with aged cheese.

Your father's teeth: They are mine, too.

And your daughter's belly is on your plate;
you pulled it from my bones.

Pluck from it the gallstones of your wife
like you are searching for pearls.

What is that strange taste in your mouth?
Your sister's spleen? Bitter and juicy?

Take my body
in paper sacks to the butcher;
get the best flavour from each cut.

Grind my jaw and pelvis to powder;
brush your teeth with me.

Don't worry: Soon you will be
the run-off of my decay.

SCRYING

An offering to Biddy Early, Wise Woman of Clare

1

Mummy, I breathe you in,
stroke the grave cloth that swaddles you,
the way you taught me to swaddle my dolls
in old dishrags.
I stroke your hair, brittle with the hunger
that wracked you with a certain eagerness,
a wish to crawl deep into the ground.
To burrow—
like a worm,
a mole.

Mummy, I breathe you in,
but it is not your scent
that weaves round my nasal cavities
like a spider's web
or a flame.
It is the stench of uncooked meat
left too long on the counter in the summertime.
It is the thick stench of dust and the sweet wickedness
of old leaves and flowers in mud.
This stench is not you
but I drink it still,
clutching your body as it grows colder and colder.
We do not have anything to start a fire and keep warm
so I shiver against you,
we are together in your death bed.

2

In the doctor's study
I sort bottles by the intent of their contents,
the amount of dust gathered
on the coloured glass.
I empty the bedpans onto wet grass and stir
cubes of sugar into his tea,
lick my fingers.
I ask him how to cure a chill, a cough,
a crackling in the chest.
Starve it, he says, *to death.*

3

The poorhouse is cold, damp stone.
I share a single bed with three other girls,
their hearts stunned moths
against my limbs, their skin taut,
bones ripe with want.
The blanket leaves rough red patches around my neck—

a choking itch that blooms in the night.

4

I told Pat we could marry, that
I'd rather sleep with him than a stranger's piss
in my sheets.
(Romantic as it is not.)
His heartbeat is buried deep in his man-body.
No part of him is bird-brittle,
or insect-like.
No part of him will sluice off,
or snap.

5

I took Tom into my arms,
let him coo at his father's grave before
brushing his hair with thistle
and kissing his orphan teeth.

6

I lay next to a man who is not mine by blood,
not a son. Truly
a lover, a stepson,
step-lover—

a steppingstone to another life.

We stretch ourselves over one another,
like a screen to block out the black flies.
All day and night I answer the door, wrap wool blankets
around frost-bitten feet,
anoint clammy foreheads with rosewater
and melted sleet.

John stirs and snorts in his sleep and I busy myself
by the stove, stirring and stirring and
a paste of comfrey and slipper greases my forearm—
where the neighbour's dog bit down.

When I raised my fist the beast
swung from me like a hanged man.

I could not heal it.

7

When I was young
and talked to the fairies,
I did not see in the pool of my future
a busy house and an empty body.

One child mine, and one son-child-husband,
a parlour full of men drinking
and women drowning.

All the while the sting of the nettle hung round my neck
like a string of pearls,
or a noose.
I vowed never to be a servant girl again.

8

I married for a third time,
restored a crumbling spring well so that the village butter
could wet the bread
and fry the fish
and grease the wheels.

But somehow I feel that the hounds and the heifers
I've healed
are angry and leeching from me
a blood that fuels the priests' rage.

Tonight I curl into myself,
into the well, into this bed of wet stone
and sleep without a husband to wake me,
a knock to spring me out of bed,

or a fairy to crawl into my ear and tell me
to slather the newborn babes with honey.

9

I could not cross the river to defend myself.
It was swollen with summer rains
when my last husband died.
They called me the devil's familiar,
the fairy's apprentice.

It's not my fault the landlord died half in,
half out the window, or that my husband
drank more than three horses in August.

I know what the blue bottle tells me
and I know that in my dying days they'll praise me,
priests and all, for they are only sour now,
only sorrowful because they cannot sew a person whole
with meadowsweet and a stiff whiskey.

Holy water and hymns alone
are not enough.

THEY SAID IT WOULD NOT HARM
THE DELICATE TISSUE

I was a wife,
full of buttercup and custard;
poised, a jewel
spilling tulle
from my ears.

I was a sister,
a field of crushed blackberries;
fell pregnant for the twelfth time.
It bubbled,
it burnt,
I bled, I shed.

I was a mother,
an elocutionist versed
in the language of stinging tear ducts
and hangnails.

I was a sister;
grandmother's diamond ring
rested easy in my cervix,
wrapped in wax
and acid, a Christmas tree ornament.

I was a daughter, told
this is essential to your marriage bed
this cream cleanser will take years off

your porcelain tub, shave decades
from your indifferent web.

I was a woman
sleepwalking
sleep-bleeding
sleep-burning
sleep-eating
myself whole.

HAT BOX

For Lucy Maud Montgomery

Earliest memory: mother in coffin,
the tubercular bed I grew in.
A haunted wood: I thought the birch
was the monarch of our forest
but it was mother's grave that ruled.

In the fairy room I split in two,
by Maiden Lake I became a tree.

At Journey's End on Riverside Drive,
my bark flaked off. In dreams, I
held my baby hand to
mother's cheek and Hugh's purple
thimble-hands tore out my hair.

Barbiturate spells place me inside
that old hat box where I locked up
my sugar stories
and grief.

Like a tree
I am losing my leaves.

PROJECTIONS OF A GLASS WOMB

1
During the virgin state
the passage
abounds with rungs
or wrinkles, to be much altered
or obliterated
by child-bearing.

> 2
> The covering
>   is smooth
> and unbroken in the young
>   but in age
>   becomes covered
>   with scar-like marks
> that respond
>   to the silky substances
>   within.

3
The ovaria
are tied
each by a short
ligament
to the bottom
      of the uterus,
          the membrane
            of the belly.

4

The belly, a theatre,
embraces the interior bones
in such a manner
that they can be felt by the fingers,

the principal object of touching,
the dense membrane; true skin
the inferior / the
interior.

5

The flood, red,
    and alarming
  swallows
    the silence
      between thighs.

6

The patient is to be
kneeling, stooping forward
on her elbows,
one hand
introduced into the vagina,
the other into the rectum,
to produce such pressure
as may prove successful.

7
The dam does not break—
the waters do not spill,

fragments held by makeshift walls
float, uneasy,
full of burnt lotus—
a black storm inside.

8
The children struggle
within,
come out
red all over,
like a hairy
garment.

9
When the cord
is broken, there is softness again.

10
Like a crimson pickle,
the child has long
eyelashes.
They glisten.

11
The birth
lingers, and
makes the scalp
swell with rude violets.

12
Lungs, unexpanded
    and heavy
  sink
   in water,
   swimming.
An infallible mark
   that the child
  is born alive.

13
A white crust of various thickness
excites fever
softened by opiates and Borax.
Mercury may be administered
to a girl exposed to venereal
poison that appears
soon after birth—
as blotches,
crusts
& ulcers,   t h r u s h.

THIS IS WHERE THE HOUSE STOOD

                              before I took a match to it,
                    watched the ashes
              leap into the January sky.
The smell of gasoline
still makes my ear canals itch.

Mother called me a bitch,
so I cut her up,
tossed her to a ditch.
Brother called me foul,
so I pulled out his bowels,
fed them to the pigs.
Father screamed at me every day
so I stabbed him in the neck,
hid his body under the deck.

This is where the house stood
before I took an axe to it.
The stone foundations remain—
charred black and stacked
like bones sticking in mud.

Father was a mad sort,
mother was a cow,
brother was an ugly thing
suckling at the sow.

This is the marrow of the house;
the ashes black and dusty.
The whole damn thing
was rusted,
bleak, and altogether rotten.

Once there was a house here,
it held a family in its bowels.
They groaned and gurgled day and night,
they made the milk go sour.

WHISKERS

Between classes I haunted the vault of the University of
Calgary archives where I worked as a grad student.
I lingered, always, by the first editions of Plath and Sexton.
Like a luck charm I'd run my finger along the tip of a
badger's whisker that Ted Hughes taped into a hand-stitched
chapbook shelved next to an early edition of *The Colossus*.

One day I will run my fingers along the marbled spine of
the box at the Lily Library that contains Sylvia's hair shorn
in childhood, hair that never felt Ted's brute fingers.
I wonder if Ted plucked those whiskers from a badger
in the wild, its thick musk like Sylvia's heavy memory.

But no, Ted couldn't touch a woman without cowering in
his study, never mind a wild animal. He always did like to
pluck bits and pieces from the dead as they lay helpless.

WASHERWOMAN

The pond moves with darkness
and crusted blood.
The rumblings of something breathing,

something beating,
flit deep within me.
In the dark I wash the stains from cloth;

the blood collects in the pond.
By morning it will have dried
and left a dusty copper ring.

This is the most earnest washboard;
it catches the light of the moon.
I made it from an ash,

carved it inch by inch with my teeth,
sanded it down with my breath.
My mother died in childbirth,

washed my bloodied sheets
when the calf fled from my thorny womb
sixteen years later.

Like a moth in the corner of the hospital room,
she hovered and wept at the placental dew.
I hang my weeping organs on a clothesline;

like my mother before me,
continue to wash the worn
and womb-stained linens.

On washboards made of ash and bone,
I scrub the blood and dirt
from the grave clothes of my lovers.

This is the most earnest washboard,
it is lacquered
with the wetness of keening.

My mother has served her sentence,
so I wash alone now, wait for passersby
to help with the wringing of the linens.

Three twists clockwise, their arms
will rip from their sockets, giving me
two more hands for washing.

Three twists counter-
clockwise and they have
nine years to live.

The pond moves
with darkness
and crusted blood.

I sit back on a stone, watching
thirty-three arms
do my earnest washing.

PHOSSY JAW

This match can be lit anywhere.
Strike it on a book
or the rough wood of your kitchen table.
Let the glow of the flame
brighten those dark London streets!

I bought a frozen charlotte doll for my daughter—
three days' wages
for a piece of porcelain in a matchbox bed.

The little matchstick girl died in the cold without a coat,
but did she glow like me?

My daughter kept the doll beneath her pillow
while she slept. I looked in on her,
holding a chunk of my own flesh in my hand,
my jaw a rotting socket.

She slept so very peacefully, but the corner
of my eye was a yellow light
I couldn't quite catch.

MOORWITCH

Some nights she smothers rabbits with freshly laundered
silk sheets. A ritual held since childhood: each fortnight
a tincture, white and thick like curdled milk. The
powder from a stolen skull sinks into her stomach.

Each waning gibbous she feeds the mother rabbit
foxglove. The poison leaks envious onto her tongue.
She slips pokeweed into ears of the kits.

Outside, the children chase each other with sharp sticks,
and the kits palpitate before depleting and she trips down
the bank, her ankles coated in creamy silt,

the thick
            white pus that seeped

from the mother rabbit's eyes.

She cannot cry; she sends the bodies of the babies down
the stream in wicker coffins. She picks stinging nettle
and fashions it into a gown. She picks hemlock and
fashions it into a suit. The stuffed body of the poisoned
mother rabbit officiates the Moorwitch's wedding to a
scraggly hare

in the clearing
            across the river.

THIS LITTLE WORLD

The Winchester Mystery House, San Jose, California

Sarah, the imp of your womb is gold-plated,
a chicken-footed infant,
all bones and pockmarked with missing
feathers.
She'll make a decent stock for stew.

The violet and blue glass
refracts her years, splicing memory
like meat.

Did your womb crumble like the tower,
Sarah? Seize and contract,
trap you
like a fallen wall?

Is this house your twisted organ, Sarah?
Did you sit curled up in a room
full of steam and fire—
to try to bring the salamanders back,
revive the frozen reptiles inside you?

Did you adopt the ghosts like ferrets?
Cage birds like stolen children
dressed in their Sunday best?
Flicker
in the basement with the rats?
Crawl up the coal chute to say hello to the wasps?

Did you grind her tiny, starving
body into mica—
to glimmer forever in the crystal bedroom?

THE DERRYMAQUIRK WOMEN

In the mud, there are stories of women and foxes
and the yellow flowers that adorn their bodies.

Bring your bones to me, I say, and
with a flick of my tongue I will watch you fall.

Hold out your hand, I will read your fortune
with a flick of my wrist; your wounds are packed with
goldenrod.

Hold this leech to your cheek, your eyes grow wide.
With a suck I drain your abscess.

In the mud, there are stories of women and foxes
and the yellow pus they drain from the bog cutters.

Languid, they heal and fell the men
and sink back into the peat to tend to their infants.

ANOTHER RESURRECTION

After Saint Christina the Astonishing

Some women sleep on silk sheets.
I prefer thickets of thorn bushes caressing my thighs,
the whirring of waterwheels, the thrill of near-drowning.
I find solace in bread ovens; the smell outside is too much
like dirty rags, a virgin sipping milk from her pert tit.

Watch how I quiver in my skin all night, the patron saint
of the woebegone, the winsome, the wild.
Watch how I fling dirt upon my face to become wretched
        like you.
I have fits in front of the tabernacle, leap from the grave to
lick the clouds.

I bite my skin to show you what fear tastes like.

AT THE ULSTER MUSEUM

After Stephen Sexton

A little girl with frilled pink socks
and daisies in her braids
crawls into the stump of a plastic tree
to call a gleeful *hello!*

Hello hedgehog!
Hello little mouse!
Hello mister owl!

Fairy doors open
to reveal a stuffed finch on plastic moss,
a field mouse hiding its glass eyes
from the sticky fingers of children.

Everything here is for touching
a curator sings.
Snow White with an electronic security pass,
taxidermy princes and plastic play sets.

Three fox cubs curled together,
eyes glued shut—
like stillborns.

The little girl with the frilled pink socks
and pinch-red cheeks wonders
why the animals lie so silent.

Everything here is for touching,
the living, the dead
and the in-between.

A bushy tail
hangs like a feather duster,

the girl plays tug-of-war with the plastic tree,
reaches to pet a hedgehog and squeals
at the spines
scraping her flesh-ripe palm
before running to mummy.

Everything here is for touching.

II.

*"The breath of my grandmother's garden
is inside my ears."*

AXE TIDINGS

One should never bring hawthorn blossoms indoors.
Bessie's mother knew this but insisted.

The sun was hot on Bessie's back.
The box was heavy like a body.

One by one she dropped the silver knives
into the well.

It echoed hollow,
smelled like mildew.

Bessie dreamt of a wedding, her grandmother's
lace gown illuminated by white candles
held up by wax.

The groomsmen were crows.
The bridesmaids were hares.

One by one she dropped her sister's pearls
into the well.

Thursday last an adder slithered under the porch light,
something had to be done.

One by one their fingers fell,
followed by the axe
down the well.

UNSUITABLE

1
I plant offshoots of aloe
in broken jars.

The mother, a beast of a plant,
is an offshoot herself, a relic
of my first home.

The matriarch of all aloes sleeps like the luck dragon
in the corner of my grandmother's kitchen,

soft and spiny and oozing
over my brother's sunburnt neck.

I whisper secrets to these new buds:

There are bodies in the horse pasture,
there are teeth
sprinkled like eggshells into the moist soil,

lumps of soil covering shoe boxes,
makeshift crosses with misspelt names.

I turn the broken bits over in my fingers,
in their discount potting soil,
the new blooms are happy
enough.

2

One of the plants will not take to the new soil.
It sits on my desk next to a jar of pens.
I prop it up with a toothpick crucifix, pray
it will live.

With a fork I extract all hints of mould
from my herb garden.
(But if the mould is black,
insidious, how can I find it in the mud?)

I kiss the tips of petals.
The breath of my grandmother's garden
is inside my ears, whispering
dying spells:

Run with the dandelions
and don't let your husband
clean his gun in front of you.

Children, keep the weapons
far from the bed.

Turn the autumn leaves
into mulch and feed me.

I am hungry, feed the gaping
hole in my cheek.

3

I water the jade on the bedside table with
my husband's unfinished midnight water.
It smells acidic,
like his hot breath
bleaching holes

                down my back
        as we
sleep.
I hope it doesn't kill the plant.

4

I once found kittens abandoned by the side of the road,
put them in a basket by the radiator for warmth.
I fed them milk from my fingertips,
but only one survived.
My husband
returning home,
kicked his steel-toe boots into their nest.

The survivor loved the holly plant
on the bookcase
(which killed it
in the end).

5

Each night I soak in scalding water,
watch my stomach bloom a fat lip.

6

I live with my body arching
always, to something that smells of dirt.

My lips graze the heads of the blooms that
burst
from the glistening centre of a plant
whose name I can't remember.

Each time I walk past the pantry I inhale
the sweetness of the hanging garlic from the family
garden.
Sometimes
I give away the plants but mostly
I keep collecting, and the plants keep growing
and the skin
of my hands grows soft from the aloe—
pricked from roses,
fragrant from garlic.

7

Now there is mould in the spine of my favourite book.
I sip my coffee and with a
rag torn from an old shirt, I scrub
and scrub and the mould is clear
and black now, spreading
through the house, up the windows
over the radiators, into the mattress.

I want to lie in bed all day,
breathe in the dying
fern on the nightstand; watch the squirrels

cling to the tree,
their autumn bellies pulling them
into the wind, making the wiry branches
    flip
        and
    turn.

I think of the kitten, how it died with a belly
bruised with holly,
its ears twitching, eyes glazed over,
sucking on a leaf
held loose in my hand.

8
The porcelain doll
fell behind the refrigerator.
I found the kitchen to be unsuitable
for resurrection,
my arms too short to facilitate a rescue mission.

Now she lies
with fruit flies. I picture her cracked ceramic face
turned upwards, away from my fingers
feeling for her.

When I found her at the antique shop,
she cried out
from the bookcase,

    Mama! Mama!

I shrank from motherhood,
let her fall to the dust bunnies,
into the space where the dustpan empties.

By the time my husband returned
with arms like fishing nets,
I'd found a replacement
and brushed her plastic hair.

9
I miss the cat,
her thistle tongue lapping cream
from old dishes,

shaking dander into the sink—
that silken seasickness
of feline humours,
familiar whine of the familiar.

I eat soup and rosemary twigs
while wind bludgeons the eaves.

I ache for a companion,
un-rooted in pinch-pots of soil,
un-rooted in matters of flesh.

10
November. My desk
overflows with scraps:
obituaries torn from the newspapers,
coupons for fireworks,

receipts from the hardware store—
we needed new knives.

I sleepwalk and leave water stains on the hardwood.

There's a chip out of each mirror in the house.
It's my fault.

I drift off to the gurgling knock of the radiator,
the sleep-scattered smell of my husband gulping the night.

When I lurch in my dreams
with my spit-drenched hair—
like a rat he curls into my body.

I feel the chill seep under the covers
on days when I am the last to leave our bed,

my pillow a valley of crumbs, and
I soak in oil till the witch-knots in my neck
come loose

I miss the sun on my face—my aorta is
an icicle stretching through me—into the frozen ground.
I want to swim in hot tea,

stay in a hotel with blankets warm from the dryer.

I shiver in the bathtub, holding whiskey in earl grey to
         my chest

till he comes home to breathe
wet heat onto my toes.

Winter wastes me.

11
In my nightmares the walls of the library
swallow up the office where I used to work.
The university landscape shifts,
tilts and throws me into the wrong places
at the wrong times.

All my students are clear silicone cases
filled with yellow, bloodied teeth.
They scream at me
over their midterm grades.
The teeth swell
with abandoning rattle.

12
I find a shoe in the black snow
—a child's Hello Kitty sneaker, pink
like newborn gums,
it lights up when I nudge it.

I wonder if it contains a small child
nestled as in a crib.

It glows in the sludge, a
Jack-o-lantern.

I pick it up by the wet lace,
toss it in the dumpster.

My grandmother always said,
Ask no questions
when disposing of bodies.

Later, in the dark
I rummage for the shoe, the beacon
in the trash, and bring it home, scrub it clean.
Place it at the heart
of the luck-dragon aloe.

13
I wake in stiff sweat, knocking
cups off the mustard table;
the radiator yells in the hollow basement.

Concrete and copper arteries slam
silver blood around the house.

I am a giant caterpillar,
winding around these hardwood floors,
staring at myself in the warped glass
of the front windows,
waiting for the rot to freeze,
or spring.

14
A bleak frost seals the compost bin shut.
The pumpkin a smiling rind with splintered
toothpick teeth.

A glass breaks,
pops in the dishwater. I
sift through the soapy wet to collect the bits,
shove the evidence into my pockets.

The shards dig into my hips.
I peel my jeans off, sit
in the empty tub. Waiting

for the aphids to nest between my toes,
for a mossy ache, for ivy to crawl up my damp
back,
till I'm overgrown.

Later I hear the shards
tinkling around the barrel of the clothes-dryer.

I pull them, one-by-one from
the warm fabrics,
kiss the broken pieces;
by the firelight
mourn my sharp edges.

15
I wait for the rabbits
to turn brown
again,
and for the trees to suck their leaves
up from the ground, for the ditches to
unpack the weight—waste of winter.

My myrtle, brittle in her purple pot,
sheds her tiny leaves like toenail clippings.

I miss the cat, sometimes.
My students, rarely.

I placed two dying ferns in the compost
last night, tossed two moulding
sourdough loaves over their sad figures.

I remember that all plants die,
that winter is a rash:
dry   itching   mottled.

The crooked glass of the front room
is eighty years old.
It holds in the heat;
the light filters through
like the face of a lake.

I live off of what's contained
in this house:

an air plant,

a fairy doll in a coffin

buried in the side of

Arthur's Seat.

BLACK BOOTS

She perches on a stool in the kitchen.
A fat raven with legs too long and spidery
for her body.
She watches her mother ease the paper skin
off the onions, shedding the copper flakes
and the fragrant soil
onto the tile floor.
The little girl's black boots
are knocking, knocking, knocking
on the metal-framed stool,
its scaffold a rusty skeleton
holding her suspended in the open warmth
of the bread oven.

Her mother comes at her with a small pair of scissors,
rusted from sitting in the sink.
Shrieking like a dull axe or golden scalpel,
her mother places
a sliver of bay leaf on her forehead,
ties
a butcher's knot into her boot laces

after she takes the yellowed lace tablecloth from the closet
to ready the table
for Sunday roast.

BLOODLETTING

Mary, I will care for your leeches and I
will not say that you possess me. I will not call you
a wonder, or claim to be your beating heart.
Mary, I will kiss your leeches and when I am hurt,

I will feed them with my blood. There are no
demons in our bodies or our minds, but yes,
yes, it feels as if there might as well be. This
disease is a burning, a bruising, a bleeding.

Bleed with me, Mary. Bleed with me
till the shaking stops and the wind settles and we
are no longer leeched dry by our own brains.
Bleed with me, Mary. We are already so tired.

THE PURPORTED LAST WORDS OF RUTH BLAY

Tell me where I'll be hanged.
The elm? The gallows? The balcony
of my lover's home?
Don't let my students watch, don't
let the girls see. I haven't yet
taught them what it means to be

a woman. They don't know the weight
of an infant dead and peeking up through
the slats in the floor. Let them live quietly
for now. I'll visit them in their dreams,
tell them of this pain when they are ready.

Tell me where I'll be hanged.
I'm not the first and I won't be the last—
we girls in barns give birth to
burdens, these burdens
lie planted beneath the floor—
like mandrakes for unwed mothers.

Tell me where I'll be hanged, I'll
wear my Sunday best to the unmarked grave.
Tell me where I'll be hanged and when it's over
I'll lay an altar to the child who stopped kicking
seven months in.

Burn an effigy of me and warn the girls
that this is what becomes of us—women
who want, women who watch, and
women who wander.

Warn them: Motherhood is death.
Spinsterhood is death. Death is the colour
of menstrual blood and breast milk.

Warn them.

THE MOUTH OF LYNNHAVEN

It is said that witches ride in eggshells downriver
to deliver babies out of wedlock, under cover of night,
that witches turn into hares to escape the grasping fingers
of men with scythes for eyes and briars for tongues.

Of the truthfulness of these two things I do not know,
but I do know that when they ducked Grace Sherwood in
the water, with a thirteen-pound bible tied to her neck,
she sputtered to the surface
and spat in the faces of her accusers.

THE FARMHAND'S GIRL

The knots on the old barn door are an off-black
black, also the dirt on my gardening gloves—
limp in a broken flowerpot.

How frost, feeling bold, braids itself into my hair,
eager and lonely our lovemaking on the porch,
the leaves felled on muddy gravel.

Children with dusty sweaters climb the trees.
The tent waits folded in the storage shed—
moon's milk, the ground's copper eyelids.

The black knots of the dirt road,
the night seamless,
the old door, bleeding sap and glue, splits.

Against the wall of the barn,
the gardening gloves, a floral pattern,
are fouled with dirt, the flesh of worms.

The new light bares its low moan—
the corrosive air of September.
My skin cracks with cold, the beets I did not taste.

I lick the dirt for one last night.

GIRLS WHO COULD DO NO WRONG

When she was born
the orchards lost their tidiness,
the town became overgrown,
the wind blew with a shrill urgency
every night of her infancy.

Her mother, long dead
(a copper tub, a rope) told her:

You are my little girl,
no matter what, you can do no wrong.
Look over your left shoulder as you go,
see your death; a silk rose in its neat frame.

Her children take off their shoes at the front entrance,
stand in their stiff socks. It is the middle of February
and she feels like a ghost.

Her red curls, like a house fire,
cast a spell on the town. She's in the pond
and knows she'll never lie again.

Some places grow old peacefully.
She thinks of herself pregnant seven times,
their days numbered, her mother gone.

She holds her daughter in the death-cold pond,
the child kicks through the ice,
head bouncing against the underside

of the skating rink,
till the ice blooms red and she sings:

You are my little girl,
no matter what, you can do no wrong.
Look over your left shoulder as you go,
see your death; a silk rose in its neat frame.

CHARLOTTE

A china girl sleeps
in a matchbox bed;
frozen,
her tender bones tumbled smooth
to flesh-round stumps.

NUPTIAL FLIGHT

The world is a garden translated by fire.
A female says yes by closing her wings,

and the blueberries push their lush spice.

The Cabbage White is a minimalist.
She says no by fluttering her wings.

Butterflies have a fate, their displacement
green and sympathetic.

Somewhere in Europe
the flowers want a good listener—
the chanting of the blueberries, not quite the song
of pretty swallows.

The Holly Blue holds grudges.

The sky is a map pinpointed with ducks
who nip at butterflies, only out for a lay.

Since the glands of virgins have little smell,
they suckle fresh blueberries to draw others in.

Let the male collect the alkaloids;
the female holds her wings tight to her back
like shoulder blades.

The female has enough work to do, now.

CONFESSION

When Frances followed the little thing into the shallow
beck, I stayed back, watching her stockings sag in the
water, flapping at her ankles like second skins. Frances
batted her eyelashes and the imp trusted her.

I wished to catch it and place it in a box like a pet in a
spider-silk dress, pull it out at parties to flutter and tease
and spit. When Frances giggled as its wings tickled her
rosebud cheek, I confess:

I wanted to hold its gossamer body in my palm, knowing
I could crush it with my breath. The waters of the beck
leaked into my shoe, the cold water like tiny elfin teeth
biting my toes. A gasp and—Oh!

The thing is dead. Caught under Frances' fat palm;
she slipped on a patch of moss.

The photos may be fake, but the fairies—

They were real.

Weren't they, Frances?

BEAUTIFUL BAIT

A man who looked like Michael Cleary
wrapped his lips around me like
I was a changeling he needed to devour,
and in that dark cabin
I felt his hot lips running down my body,
his body hovering like a raincloud
leaking molasses into my navel.

A man who looked like Michael Cleary
pulled out tufts of my hair and placed them in the fire.
We walked naked over sharp rocks,
he pushed me into the shallow waters
to cool my burns.

A man who looked like Michael Cleary
held me under
until my burns flaked into the river.

BED, LAKE

The colicky child cried into the lake.
The lake, beginning to overflow with spring rain,
rose up to the tree line, weeping.

The mother in the flannel nightdress
sank, her knees
muddy with the colicky child's screams.

A colicky lake, a four-poster bed,
a weeping child, a muddy mother,
all soaking with spring rain.

Alongside wooden paths by the lake,
the ants ate away at the steps,
the mother swam with her child in the storm.

The calm cracking of distant lightning,
the lake pulling the flannel nightdress,
counting the child's toes.

The child sprang up, the mother sank, the
lake swirled them wet in a dance.

The child's teeth bit through his gums.
Floating above the lake,
his mother sound asleep in the four-poster bed.

ROOM

Hunger as blank as a burnt book
capsizes me.
Each hour the nurse
takes my breasts
and microwaves them in time for tea
in the break room.

Mother looks on with sunken cheeks
and bites at edges of her nails.
I stare at the nurse with her missing lashes.
Did you pull them out, hair by hair?

Bread is sinister,
I spit into the sink.
Breadcrumbs mingle with my dead skin
in the bed sheets that should be burnt.
I spit into the sink.
Bread
is the sludge thickening around the base of my spine.
I spit into the sink.

Mother looks on with sunken cheeks
and bites at edges of her nails.
I stare at the nurse with the missing brows.
Did you pluck them out, follicle by follicle?

Milk is yellow and clumpy,
like my wasted hair in the washbasin.
I am no churchyard,

but my fingers reach like skeleton keys
to the crypts; I spit in the sink.
Never again will milk dribble from my chin
or leak from my breast,
seep from the corner of the cat's eye.
Never again will the moon be the colour of old milk
on a dark September morning.
I spit into the sink,
beg mother to stop chewing at her fingers.

NEST-BODY

When she comes in through the hotel window,
moths flock to her.
They flutter against her shoulders,
sip on her breasts,
drawing out honey with their eyes.
The wildflowers creep up her legs.
There are flat stones under her feet,
a strange hand on her back.
His fingers are rough from running
through her,
fingering the bark on her chest.

She runs farther each day,
curses further each day
he forces her to run with babies
clutching her lungs till she succumbs.

With her sisters she hangs naked
from the roof-beams of ill-intentioned men.
Blood-soaked, their shadows
strike corvus across the ground.

Men flock to her.
When she comes in through the chimney,
they rip her hair from her head
with their teeth,

suck and suck on her empty breasts.
She crushes them in their sleep,
heels forced into eye sockets.

Feel them.

III.

*"... depth of unmarked women
made of wire."*

WITCHING

Are you dancing in the skin of your brother?
Is that your skull in the Wytch Elm?
Are you cold out there,
Bella?
Is the milkmaid's collarbone growing
hot against your thigh?
Does it hurt
to breastfeed pet foxes
with sharp teeth.

FLICKERS

The trees have wings
and witches are gathering
around the elms.

This tree has a hole between its wings
where cracked moths lie
dusted among the particles.
The newer branches are
lighter with the bark stretched.

This tree has catered
to zealots, to maids,
to rabbits and corpses,
helped spiders spin silk to dusky hands,
its lichen grabbing
at masses of dead skin;
till now,

until this gathering.

The witches are mourning
this trunk. Its tumours
tremor, a century of use.
The staunch, severed leaves
black as charred meat.

The tree has a wing;
long, split silver.
Bleak like raw chicken;

the beast now just a small body,
her dusty shimmer,
flimsy in a cloud of dust
or mosquitos
crumbling
into the ground.

Who put Bella in the Wytch elm?
We did.

BIRTHMOTHER

My tigress perfume
enters the burnt parlour
of the old woman's home.

It smells like rhubarb and moths.

I notice her breasts,
their sag and the stale jag
of the scar from the corner of her mouth
to her chin. On
the mantle is a photo of her
in stockings;

my small sick pulse darkens and twists.
She says, with her Glasgow smile
and caterpillar teeth,

"You may have a baby someday;
depending
on the juicy starch, the
petting, parking,
the landscape."

The old woman passes me fruit
on a copper plate,
arranged in a waxing moon.
The sharp fragrance of stale
oranges tears open her scar.

The early strawberries
are the exact colour of fresh blood
plucked from their vines.

Her gnarled white roots of hands
curl around my ear lobe. Her
black moss hair is steel wool
scrubbing the dirt off my cheeks.
"You may have a baby someday,"
she chalks into my ear,
"but not
while the contamination
is in the clockwork
of the womb,
not
while this house is still breathing,
while I'm still breathing."

She sucks on plastic fruit,
spitting as she speaks.
The old woman whispers my name.
"You may have a baby someday,
but I,
I will not."

JANE

You will sit amongst the wild,
reluctant.

Sleeping next to you, a doe,
a blistered doe,

lips blue,
a young, blackened doe—

whimpering, illuminated by the streetlights—a dream,
and a lake like a slice of fat,
white in the dark under lights.

Here you are a bruised pear.
And I thought I loved you, your thick fingers,
the wet forest of it all.

You slip in
and I find I am a cavern; you the velvet worm.
It is sad for me
to be explored, to sleep with a fetid pear in my mouth—

to feel the mush of your damaged bits against my lips
in the alley,
the damp mushrooms,
the frantic mice, the yellow mould.

Our reckless flesh
draped over concrete—
a broken man and his doe
drained of blood, white
like a mannequin,

or a Christmas decoration.

BONE DAZZLER

After Quinta Maggia McDonald

She worked long, glowing hours,
painting numbers,
licking paint.

She wasn't there to catch
the reluctant pearls
of her daughter's milk teeth
as they fell out;

but Quinta's teeth,
that once clutched rags as she pushed
that small body from hers,

shook themselves loose
from her mottled jaw
and moth-eaten, she collected them
from the factory floor,
placed them into a small green bottle

later; in an attic trunk,
a child's rattle.

ICE FISHING IN MAY

Antagonistic,
smug in broken lace.
A blossoming,
a hard leather shell,
peroxide limbs swathed in vitiligo.

The sea women wither with their pearl nooses
weighed down with heavy scrim,
over and over the bloat still floats,
calm and putrid as a swollen cloud.

A blank smile,
the porcelain crack
down a waterlogged face,
the foaming stench of the bombyx.
The dark green forest beneath the waves,
the thorns sprouting from the corpses,
sharp teeth dulled by tide.

Stockings heavy, knocking against the floor of the lake.

The weeds attend them like overblown infants,
their hair heavy wet wool—
no screaming, no clawing,
just stillness.
There are no rocks in the pockets
of their frocks, no iron chains.
Only stillness, the cool water
grey
and reassuring.

CURSE OF CASSANDRA

We are broken china with snakes painted on our flanks
in gold leaf.
We are the nails in your coffin.
We are the dead peacocks in your garden.
We decorate your crowns with turquoise blood.

The tomb seals like Tupperware.
And our feet?
Our feet have ears.
And our tongues?
Our tongues are laurels.
We tear your fingernails out with our prophecies,
your last rites are written in butcher string
tacked to an old pine tree.
We are the shoebox
that you placed your dead cat in
and threw to the moor.

Holiness
is a slippery fish.
We are the scales flaking into the fire.

You never believed us in the first place.

CROW THEORY

After Bella Wright

They will say that a crow gorged itself to death
on my blood,
stumbled into a field and died from its gluttony
before they will say
that a man could have bled me dry,
stared me down with a gun
without first hurting me
in different ways.

RED BIRD IN WINDOW

They said the blood would go away
and stay there, like father.

I have a pair of silk boots,
but I do not like the way the stockings stick to my prickly legs.

In the display window
the violin whines from my lap—
old, it leeches water, cracks down the back.
My son weeps in harmony,
I scratch at the bumps on my scalp.

My eyes feel like blood clots.
I undress,
splash water between my legs,
tear open my corset so my child can feed.
My husband feels my wretched beat.

Ferns lap at my chest like soft waves
and I lie on a straw bed, a woolen blanket—

my family a yellowing nativity scene
through frosted glass.

My adopted name sits on my chest like silt
and the angle of my wrist writes maps on the baby's back
and my husband breathes into my elbow
and the wax paper window lets them look in—
grey with body sweats and the dust of living.

MISTRESS

A soldier dug up my corpse.

Bloated   it floated
in her arms   in the wet   in the dark.

She carried me to the forest
to dig a fresh grave,
to sew me back up with winter creeper
pulled from the trunk of a Wytch elm.

She lay down next to me   held on to me,
     breathed over me
like I was a relic
adorned with precious metals
and she a crypt keeper—

until the morning light sent her
     not home   back   into battle.

I sleep safe in my new tomb   my new womb.

BIRDBONES

A wicker basket is not a womb
and I am not a girl.

Below,
lie my sisters,
in fragments, and
like tinker toys
I reassemble them.

CROSSING THE WIRES

Wire lake, threaded leaves,
six coil, black-frosted women.
When do the wire ferns that lie there die?

Our clothespins must pinch your ligament lips.

A flutter of ash flounders
above lily-shaped lungs.
The blank fox has brought us a deaf flask:

They lie round and sharp and empty, those coiled
beacons.

Heat whorls, shakes and ruptures.
The lava lives
in us, it infects the tadpoles.

A snail falls from a pale birch with peeling bark.

Books fall open, the pages soggy.
Moss grows on the words,
expressionless and black.

This is the waxen depth of unmarked women
made of wire.

SLAUGHTERING TIME

Remember me like brittle nails breaking on the notch
at the top of your spine. Remember me like blackheads,
like digging blackheads out with a needle. Remember
me like crushing blackheads between your teeth.
Remember me like jalapeños in sugar-free applesauce,
like hard-boiled egg whites with salsa and three packets
of Splenda. Remember me like sucked-on bouillon
cubes and sidewalk chalk. Remember me like a package
arriving soaked with urine on your doorstep. Remember
your affinity for anything pickled, anything hot-sauced.
Remember celery dipped in yellow mustard. Remember
wetting washcloths with the leftover water from
oatmeal, and sucking on them. Remember your mother,
crying in the bathroom at the restaurant. Remember
me like those fishnet tights and the Exacto knives.
Remember me like plain cottage cheese with relish
wrapped in iceberg lettuce. Remember your seventeenth
year, turning orange from so many carrots. Remember
me like peanut butter mixed with canned tuna and mint
sauce on soda crackers. Remember me like a purple
flower on the sidewalk; you have to eat it or it eats you.
Remember me like scraps of paper, like dead leaves, like
asking the pharmacist for a more powerful laxative.
Remember asking your mother, What is the calorie
count of Irish Spring soap?

BUCOLIC

Confession: I fell asleep by the fire last night.
It was cold and now my socks have small craters burnt into
       the toes.

Confession: I did not feed the goat
before I shut the barn door and went inside to read.

Confession: I often prod you to see if you are still stiff
       with cold.
When the temperature shifts, I worry
that your skin will slough off.

Confession: I don't bother with the walk to town most weeks.
Instead I eat the pickled onions and drink warm water
in which I've dropped egg whites.

Confession: I cross my fingers as the whites cloud in my glass
and wish for your child to leap into my womb.
The egg whites always reveal our barrenness.

Confession: I baked the following items into a cake: the left
lens from your spectacles; a molar—I can't remember
       whether it
fell from your mouth or mine; your wedding band; a quail's
       egg;
apple seeds.
The cake was large, but I ate every last bit. I swallowed
the egg whole.

After the wake, I peeled an apple in one long strip
and threw it over my shoulder. When I turned to see the
      initial
of the man I would marry next, the peel was gone.

Confession: I didn't throw it over my shoulder. I tucked it
under your head. I broke one of the church windows
and held a shard of glass under your nose to see
if there was any breath left in you.

There was not.

ROSEMARY'S LOBOTOMY

After Rosemary Kennedy

"Darling Daddy,
I hate to disappoint you in any way.
Come to see me very soon.
I get very lonesome every day."

Engulfed in tulle,
like a sprig of herb in a wedding bouquet,
she curtsied.

A stumble sideways, two seconds at most.
The crowd gasped.
The sprig of rosemary tied around her wrist
fell and rolled down the stone steps.

The nurse who delivered her
held the mother's legs shut
to try and keep the child in,
she held the infant's head in place
for seven-thousand, two-hundred seconds.

The instrument looked like a butter knife.
Rosemary carried Lilies of the Valley.
She had the flushed cheeks of a snow princess.

Deprived of oxygen, with such pressure
on the purple skin of a newborn skull,
Rosemary curdled; not much, but just enough.

The butter knife swung up and down, the procedure
"easier than curing a toothache."
She recited Wordsworth and Milton,
then nothing at all.

"Darling Daddy,
I hate to disappoint you in any way.
Come to see me very soon.
I get very lonesome every day.

A HISTORY OF TOUCHING

They say a nun in fasting is crow-like,
mildest on her back.

Full like a gull with her chest to the sea
with salt-licked teeth,

a fasting nun is ashen, like a rock-strewn shore
trapped long in herself like a spider,

crawling into muteness as ants do
and bloody as a beetroot
stolen
from the edge of the slow river.

The breasts of a nun in fasting
are mapped with blue veins that jut like bone matter,

shivering with hunger,
or desire,
or both.

NOTES

Scrying: Biddy Early (1798-1874) was a traditional Irish herbalist and healer. Landlords and local priests accused her of witchcraft. She helped local people who could not afford to go to the doctor or whom doctors had been unable to help.

They Said It Would Not Harm the Delicate Tissue: The cream cleanser referenced is Lysol. In the first half of the 20th century, Lysol products were marketed towards women as a feminine hygiene product, a douching agent and birth control. The advertisements were extremely misogynistic, shocking in their portrayal of women's insecurities. This poem utilizes the tone of these advertisements to address the reality of Lysol as a hygiene product. About 50% of women who used it to prevent pregnancy ended up pregnant, and it often caused lifelong health problems.

Hat Box: The Hugh referenced in this poem is Lucy Maude Montgomery's stillborn son.

Projections of a Glass Womb: Comprises language re-assembled and dissected from: Aitken, John. *Principles of Midwifery, or Puerperal Medicine.* Printed for J. Murray, 1786.

Washerwoman: Explores the Bean Nighe. A type of Banshee in Scottish folklore, she is an omen of death, seen washing the clothes and sheets of those about to die.

Phossy Jaw: Or phosphorous necrosis of the jaw, is an occupational disease that affected people who worked with phosphorous in unsafe conditions. Women in the 19th and early 20th centuries who worked in matchstick factories were prone to the painful disease, which caused the bone of the jaw to rot.

Bloodletting: Mary Roff (1846-1865) suffered from epileptic seizures from the age of six months till her death at nineteen in an asylum, where she was badly treated. Fourteen years after her death, Mary Roff's story was immortalized by another young woman who claimed she was possessed by Mary.

The Purported Last Words of Ruth Blay: Ruth Blay (1737-1768) was a teacher and seamstress convicted of concealing a stillborn, illegitimate infant in Portsmouth, New Hampshire, and was sentenced to death by hanging.

The Mouth of Lynnhaven: Grace Sherwood (1660-1740) was the last person convicted of witchcraft in Virginia. Known as "The Witch of Pungo," in 1706 she was subjected to "trial by water," whereby she was ducked in the river with a 5.9 kilogram bible chained to her neck.

Charlotte: "Frozen Charlotte" dolls were tiny bisque dolls, associated, in the 19th century, with tales of young women dying alone in the cold.

Confession: The speaker, Elsie Wright, is addressing her cousin Frances Griffiths. The girls became famous in the early 20th century for photographing the Cottingley Fairies;

a hoax that convinced even Sir Arthur Conan Doyle of the existence of fairies. While Elsie confessed that all five photographs were fake, Frances maintained that the fifth and final photograph was not, and that the young girls did, in fact, play with fairies in their youth.

Beautiful Bait: The man referenced in this poem, Michael Cleary, murdered his wife, Bridget Cleary by immolation in 1895 in County Tipperary, Ireland. He claimed his wife had been replaced by a changeling.

Room: Written upon hearing of the prison force-feeding of Irish Republican sisters Dolours and Marian Price. They were imprisoned for their involvement in a 1973 London bombing plot by the IRA.

Crow Theory: Bella Wright was fatally shot near the village of Little Stretton, Leicestershire on 5 July 1919. Her murder remains unsolved.

Rosemary's Lobotomy: Italicized text in this poem is from a letter from Rosemary Kennedy to her father, Joseph Kennedy (Source: *Rosemary: The Hidden Kennedy Daughter* by Kate Clifford Larson, Mariner Books, 2015).

ACKNOWLEDGEMENTS

Thank you to the editors of the following publications in which poems in this collection first appeared, some under different titles and earlier versions:

The Anti-Languorous Project: "Mistress;" "Birdbones"
APEP Publications: "Unsuitable"
Awkward Mermaid (Defunct): "Crossing the Wires"
Bad Nudes: "Red Bird in Window"
Barren Magazine: "The Purported Last Words of Ruth Blay"
Boiler Journal: "Charlotte"
Boned: A Collection of Skeletal Writings: "A History of Touching;" "Black Boots;" "The Derrymaquirk Women;" "Phossy Jaw"
Canthius: "Bloodletting"
Coffin Bell Journal: "Ice Fishing in May"
Collective Unrest: "The Mouth of Lynnhaven;" "Rosemary's Lobotomy"
Dodging the Rain: "Slaughtering Time"
Dusie, The Tuesday Poem: "At The Ulster Museum"
EVENT Magazine: "Washerwoman"
Folklore for Resistance: "Scrying"
Freefall Magazine: "Crow Theory"
Half a Grapefruit Magazine: "Flickers"
Occulum Journal: "Room"
Petal Journal: "Nest-Body"
Poethead: "Confession"
Poetry Pause: "Nest-Body"
The Quilliad: "This Little World"

Pussy Magic: "Moorwitch"
Rhythm and Bones Publications: "Another Resurrection"
Talking About Strawberries All of the Time: "Axe Tidings"
Three Drops from a Cauldron: "Bucolic"
The Warren Review: "Nuptial Flight"

Thank you to Kimmy Beach for helping me to turn a stack of poems into the first drafts of this book. Thank you to the Writers Guild of Alberta for the opportunity to be mentored by Kimmy as part of the 2019 WGA Mentorship Program.

Thank you to Alison Pick and Wayne Arthurson, writers in residence at the 2019 Writers Guild of Alberta Retreat at the Banff Centre for Arts and Creativity, where I workshopped many of these poems. Thank you to all of the other attendees for their kindness, wisdom, and inspiration.

Thank you to the staff, instructors, and fellows at the Seamus Heaney Centre: Glenn Patterson, Rachel Brown, Stephen Sexton, Doireann Ni Ghriofa, Duke Special, Leontia Flynn, Nick Laird, Edna and Michael Longley, and the late Ciaran Carson.

Thank you to Stacey Walyuchow for her incredible artist's interpretation of *Black Boots* for the People's Poetry Festival poet-artist pairing in 2018, and for inviting me to collaborate with her as part of her 2019 show *The Significance of Home.*

Thank you to Mike Thorn for being a cheerleader and first reader of this manuscript, and to Paul Meunier for encouraging and critiquing early drafts of these poems in courses at the University of Calgary. Thank you to Dania for always being willing to read strange little poems and for never allowing me to sell myself short.

Immense thanks to the Guernica Editions team: publishers Michael Mirolla and Connie McParland, associate publisher Anna van Valkenburg, designer Rafael Chimicatti, and publicists Margo Lapierre and Dylan Curran. Special thanks to Elana Wolff for her guidance and immense help with transforming this manuscript into a real-life book.

As always, thank you to my partner, Mark, and to our families for your endless love and support.

ABOUT THE AUTHOR

Erin Emily Ann Vance is the author of the novel, *Advice for Taxidermists and Amateur Beekeepers* (Stonehouse, 2019), as well as five chapbooks of poetry. She holds a Masters Degree in English Literature and Creative Writing from the University of Calgary and a Masters Degree in Irish Folklore and Ethnology from University College Dublin. Vance attended the Seamus Heaney Centre for Poetry summer course at Queen's University Belfast in July 2018 and July 2020, and was a fellow of Summer Literary Seminars in Nairobi in December 2018. She attended the Writers Guild of Alberta Banff Centre Residency in February 2019 and worked with author Kimmy Beach as part of the 2019 WGA Mentorship Program. Vance was a recipient of the Alberta Foundation for the Arts Young Artist Prize in 2017 and a finalist for the 2018 Alberta Magazine Awards for her short story "All the Pretty Bones." She is co-host of the podcast Femmes Macabres. *A History of Touch* is her first full collection of poems.

MIX
Paper
FSC® C100212

Printed in February 2022
by Gauvin Press,
Gatineau, Québec